Inspiration on the Road to Financial Freedom

Timeless Advice and
Encouragement on Achieving
Great Wealth and Financial
Success

E. J. Riordan

Copyright © 2014 My Life Coaches, Inc.

All rights reserved. No part of this publication may be reproduced, transmitted, or distributed in any form or by any means, electronic, mechanical, photocopying, recording, scanning, or otherwise without written permission from My Life Coaches, Inc.

ISBN-10: 1494911914
ISBN-13: 978-1494911911

DEDICATION

To your financial success

CONTENTS

	Acknowledgments	i
	Introduction	3
1	Goals	9
2	Positive Thinking/Positive Mindset	19
3	Discover Your Passion and Work Hard	34
4	Smart Spending	71
5	Debt	81
6	Saving	90
7	Investing	99
8	Final Thoughts	117

ACKNOWLEDGMENTS

A special thank you to Chris Jerin and Michelle Donohue for their support and guidance in this endeavor.

INTRODUCTION

The path to financial freedom, riches, tremendous wealth—or however you classify financial independence—is a goal that is firmly within your grasp. All you need to do is consistently follow a few simple truths. This book will help teach you several of those truths and provide the reinforcement needed to continue on your path to financial independence.

Library shelves are packed with thousands of personal finance books. Having read many of these throughout my career, I have discovered that each shares some basic themes, many of which I am certain you have heard before: pay yourself first, avoid credit card debt, save for a rainy day, and so on. Most of these books are exceptional and provide a clear step-by-step plan. However, like a bicycle without handlebars, we quickly find ourselves off and peddling, only to realize that we

Introduction

have no discernible control, and our plans often fall short of our desired destination.

We read the books, create what we believe to be a well-structured plan and then somehow, somewhere along the way, life gets in the way—a big project at work that becomes overwhelming, a child who falls ill, or perhaps the loss of a loved one—all life events that far too often distract us from following our well-structured plan, at least temporarily.

This book will provide you with the continual reinforcement and motivation that are crucial to staying on the path to financial freedom. It is purposefully short and to the point. It is not meant to be read straight through. Instead, I encourage reading a few quotes each day to remind yourself of and strengthen the key themes needed to help you achieve your goal. By sparing a minute or two each and every day, you will be more inclined to make better personal finance decisions and stay firmly on the path to financial freedom.

I recommend setting aside a consistent time and place each day to review a few of the quotes. I find it most useful to do this in the morning. Perhaps you will keep it near your shower and read through a couple of quotes while you wait for it to warm up. Maybe store it in your car and read through three or four quotes before you start your commute to work, school, or wherever else life might take you that day.

Introduction

As you read through the book, I suggest having a pen or highlighter handy. If you are reading this on an e-reader device you can use its highlighting and note-taking features. When you find quotes in the book that are especially motivating to you, highlight them. If you find others that are not in the book, use the blank pages at the end of each chapter or the note-taking feature on the e-reader to add these to the book.

The book is organized by each of the key ingredients that are needed to become financially successful. Ask anyone whom you consider a financial success how they achieved that success and he or she will reference many, if not all, of these, including:

1. Setting Goals
2. Positive Thinking/Positive Mindset
3. Hard Work and Passion in Your Work
4. Smart Spending
5. Avoiding Debt or Using it Strategically
6. Saving Early and Often
7. Investing

Each topic is a separate chapter, allowing you to focus on a topic that you find most relevant at a particular time, or to open the book randomly to peruse a few quotes.

Introduction

Before we jump into the lessons, let's get started with a few quotes—including some that are rather amusing—about the importance of wealth and exactly how wealth is defined by many people who have obtained it.

The definition of wealth is the number of days you can survive without physically working (or anyone in your household physically working) and still maintain your standard of living...Wealth is measured in time, not dollars.

- Robert Kiyosaki

Wealth is not without its advantages and the case to the contrary, although it has often been made, has never proved widely persuasive.

- John Kenneth Galbraith

Introduction

Money, if it does not bring you happiness, will at least help you be miserable in comfort.

- Helen Gurley Brown

When I was young I thought that money was the most important thing in life; now that I am old I know that it is.

- Oscar Wilde

Money isn't the most important thing in life, but it's reasonably close to oxygen on the 'gotta have it' scale.

- Zig Ziglar

1

GOALS

Goal setting is a consistent theme in personal finance literature. Its message reverberates in the words of anyone who teaches what it takes to be a success in anything. Want to achieve your dreams of financial freedom? You must first figure out exactly what financial freedom or financial success means to you. Is it to have $1 million in the bank or $50 million? Is it to have enough passive income to support your current living expenses or to raise your standard of living a few notches? This definition is your ultimate goal.

Once you have clearly defined your ultimate goal, you are ready to set smaller, specific, and measurable goals, with deadlines, to help get you there. These small goals will do an amazing thing. They will continually build upon one another until one day, a final small step in the process results in your achievement of the ultimate goal that you set initially.

A critical step in setting any goal is to write down the ultimate goal and the smaller intermediate goals as well. This is a must! Study after study finds that you are much more likely to achieve your goals if you write them down.

Now that you have written them down, review them frequently to keep them fresh in your mind.

The process is as simple as that. Take some time to do this now:

1. Define your overall goal.
2. Set smaller, measureable goals that lead to the overall goal.
3. Write down each goal.
4. Review your list daily.

The following quotes offer great advice on this first critical ingredient in achieving the riches you desire.

The indispensable first step to getting the things you want out of life is this: decide what you want.

- Ben Stein

The number one reason most people don't get what they want is that they don't know what they want.

- T. Harv Eker

This one step—choosing a goal and sticking to it—changes everything.

- Scott Reed

The discipline of writing something down is the first step toward making it happen.

- Lee Iacocca

There is one quality that one must possess to win, and that is definiteness of purpose, the knowledge of what one wants, and a burning desire to possess it.

- Napoleon Hill

Goals

The most important thing about goals is having one.

- Geoffry F. Abert

The secret to productive goal setting is in establishing clearly defined goals, writing them down and then focusing on them several times a day with words, pictures and emotions as if we've already achieved them.

- Denis Waitley

In the long run, men hit only what they aim at.

- Henry David Thoreau

Desires must be simple and definite. They defeat their own purpose should they be too many, too confusing, or beyond a man's training to accomplish.

- George S. Clason

Goals

Fixing your objective is like identifying the North Star—you sight your compass on it and then use it as the means of getting back on track when you tend to stray.

- Marhall E. Dimock

The difference between a goal and a dream is a deadline.

- Steve Smith

The person who makes a success of living is the one who sees his goal steadily and aims for it unswervingly. That is dedication.

- Cecil B. De Mille

Set attainable daily goals that, when achieved, provide positive reinforcement to help you stay on the path to the big goal.

- Robert Kiyosaki

Do not wait; the time will never be 'just right.' Start where you stand, and work with whatever tools you may have at your command, and better tools will be found as you go along.

- Napoleon Hill

A journey of a thousand miles begins with a single step.

- Lao-tzu

Consider the postage stamp: its usefulness consists in the ability to stick to one thing till it gets there.

- Josh Billings

The greater danger for most of us is not that our aim is too high and we miss it, but that it is too low and we reach it.

- Michelangelo

All who have accomplished great things have had a great aim, have fixed their gaze on a goal which was high, one which sometimes seemed impossible.

- Orison Swett Marden

A goal properly set is halfway reached.

- Zig Ziglar

If one does not know to which port one is sailing, no wind is favorable.

- Senec

Setting goals is the first step in turning the invisible into the visible.

- Tony Robbins

Goals

The world wasn't formed in a day, and neither were we. Set small goals and build upon them.

- Lee Haney

Our goals can only be reached through a vehicle of a plan, in which we must fervently believe, and upon which we must vigorously act. There is no other route to success.

- Pablo Picasso

Most people have no idea of the giant capacity we can immediately command when we focus all of our resources on mastering a single area of our lives.

- Tony Robbins

If you don't know what you want to do, it's harder to do it.

- Malcolm Forbes

Crystallize your goals. Make a plan for achieving them and set yourself a deadline. Then, with supreme confidence, determination and disregard for obstacles and other people's criticisms, carry out your plan.

- Paul J. Meyer

2

POSITIVE THINKING/POSITIVE MINDSET

Another theme that consistently appears in personal success and achievement literature incorporates one's mindset. Successful people report that the way they think has had a tremendous impact on the success they have achieved.

Therefore, the second area of focus to help you achieve the financial success you seek is your mindset. This includes:

1. Visualization
Visualization is critical. Frequently take time to visualize yourself as having already achieved the financial success you desire. See in your mind the high balance in your investment accounts, living in the big home, vacationing in the exotic places, quitting your job to work on something you have more passion for, or whatever else you intend to do

with that wealth. Don't be timid or shy; visualize big!

Envision yourself as a success and have sure-fire confidence you are going to achieve the wealth you want. Carry yourself as if you have already achieved the wealth you set out for. Feel the weight being lifted off your shoulders as money is no longer something you need to worry about.

2. Positive Attitude
In addition to changing your thinking and imagining yourself financially free, you must keep a positive attitude. No matter what happens, know that whatever you are going through is getting you closer to financial independence. Even if something bad is happening, find a way to put a positive spin on it and to learn from it. For example, if you lose money in an investment, take time to examine the situation and discover what the experience is teaching you that will help you in the future.

3. Mantras
Mantras are a great way to influence your thinking. Repeating a word or phrase over and over will impact your subconscious mind, which will reinforce the goals you have set to achieve and help them become reality. Examples include, "I am financially free," "I have an investment account worth $3 million," and so forth. One important note with mantras: always phrase them in a positive way. For example, say you have a lot of outstanding debt that you want to eliminate. Don't repeat "I have no

debt," as the subconscious mind does not understand the negative and will then attract debt to you. Instead, repeat, "I own all of my possessions outright," or "I have a zero balance on my credit card statement."

The quotes in this chapter will help keep your mind focused on the positive, instilling confidence that your goal of financial freedom and success will be achieved.

Nothing can stop the man with the right mental attitude from achieving his goal; nothing on earth can help the man with the wrong mental attitude.

- Thomas Jefferson

Visualize this thing you want. See it, feel it, believe in it. Make your mental blueprint and begin.

- Robert Collier

Believe you can and you're halfway there.

- Theodore Roosevelt

The size of your success is measured by the strength of your desire; the size of your dream; and how you handle disappointment along the way.

- Robert Kiyosaki

Image creates desire. You will what you imagine.

- J.G. Gallimore

The universe is transformation; our life is what our thoughts make it.

- Marcus Aurelius

You are not what you think you are, but what you think, you are.

- Brian Tracy

Wanting something is not enough. You must hunger for it. Your motivation must be absolutely compelling in order to overcome the obstacles that will invariably come your way.

- Les Brown

Let a man radically alter his thoughts, and he will be astonished at the rapid transformation it will affect in the material conditions of his life.

- James Allen

Clear your mind of can't.

- Dr. Samuel Johnson

Preceding accomplishment must be desire. Thy desires must be strong and definite. General desires are but weak longings. For a man to wish to be rich is of little purpose. For a man to desire five pieces of gold is a tangible desire which he can press to fulfillment.

- George S. Clason

Life's battles don't always go to the stronger or faster man. Sooner or later the man who wins, is the man who thinks he can.

- Vince Lombardi

Your imagination is your preview of life's coming attractions.

- Albert Einstein

Your greatest limits are not external. They are internal, within your thinking. These are contained in your personal self-limiting beliefs. These are beliefs that act as brakes on your potential. These are beliefs that cause you to sell yourself short, and to settle for far less than you are truly capable of.

- Brian Tracy

Whether you think you can, or you think you can't—you're right.

- Henry Ford

If you doubt you can accomplish something, then you can't accomplish it. You have to have confidence in your ability, and then be tough enough to follow through.

- Rosalynn Carter

Formulate and stamp indelibly on your mind a mental picture of yourself as succeeding. Hold this picture tenaciously. Never permit it to fade. Your mind will seek to develop the picture.

- Dr. Norman Vincent Peale

When a person says 'I can't afford it,' that person sees only one side of the coin. The moment you say 'How can I afford it?,' you begin to see the other side.

- Robert Kiyosaki

You can have anything you want if you want it badly enough. You can be anything you want to be, do anything you set out to accomplish if you hold to that desire with singleness of purpose.

- Abraham Lincoln

Prosperity is a way of living and thinking, and not just money or things. Poverty is a way of living and thinking, and not just a lack of money or things.

- Eric Butterworth

The thoughts we choose to think are the tools we use to paint the canvas of our lives.

- Louise Hay

Our destiny changes with our thoughts; we shall become what we wish to become, do what we wish to do, when our habitual thoughts correspond with our desires.

- Orison Swett Marden

Think positively and masterfully, with confidence and faith, and life becomes more secure, more fraught with action, richer in experience and achievement.

- Eddie Rickenbacker

Dream lofty dreams, and as you dream, so shall you become. Your Vision is the promise of what you shall one day be.

- James Allen

I visualized where I wanted to be, what kind of player I wanted to become. I knew exactly where I wanted to go, and I focused on getting there.

- Michael Jordan

Work joyfully and peacefully, knowing that right thoughts and right efforts inevitably bring about right results.

- James Allen

Your attitude, not your aptitude, will determine your altitude.

- Zig Ziglar

When you believe you can...you can!

- Maxwell Maltz

A man to carry on a successful business must have imagination. He must see things as in a vision, a dream of the whole thing.

- Charles M. Schwab

If we understood the power of our thoughts, we would guard them more closely. If we understood the awesome power of our words, we would prefer silence to almost anything negative. In our thoughts and words we create our own weaknesses and our own strengths. Our limitations and joys begin in our hearts. We can always replace negative with positive.

- Betty Eadie

Men often become what they believe themselves to be. If I believe I cannot do something, it makes me incapable of doing it. But when I believe I can, then I acquire the ability to do it even if I didn't have it in the beginning.

- Mahatma Gandhi

You must begin to think of yourself as becoming the person you want to be.

- David Viscott

Empty pockets never held anyone back. Only empty heads and empty hearts can do that.

- Norman Vincent Peale

All the breaks you need in life wait within your imagination, Imagination is the workshop of your mind, capable of turning mind energy into accomplishment and wealth.

- Napoleon Hill

The fact is, people who work the hardest do not wind up rich. If you want to be rich, you need to "think." Think independently rather than go along with the crowd.

- Robert Kiyosaki

If one advances confidently in the direction of his dreams, and endeavors to lead the life which he has imagined, he will meet with a success unexpected in common hours.

- Henry David Thoreau

If you accept a limiting belief, then it will become a truth for you.

- Louise Hay

Don't be afraid of the space between your dreams and reality. If you can dream it, you can make it so.

- Belva Davis

If you can dream it, you can achieve it.

- Zig Ziglar

You must walk to the beat of a different drummer. The same beat that the wealthy hear. If the beat sounds normal, evacuate the dance floor immediately! The goal is to not be normal, because as my radio listeners know, normal is broke.

- Dave Ramsey

We grow great by dreams. All big men are dreamers. They see things in the soft haze of a spring day or in the red fire of a long winter's evening. Some of us let these great dreams die, but others nourish and protect them; nurse them through bad days till they bring them to the sunshine and light which come always to those who sincerely hope that their dreams will come true.

- Woodrow T. Wilson

3

DISCOVER YOUR PASSION AND WORK HARD

Discovering your passion and then working hard at it is the easiest way to riches. The great news: if you love what you're doing and are having fun doing it, hard work is no longer "work." It is pure bliss!

Take time to evaluate what you really love doing. What creates "flow" or a state in which you are working on something and are completely engrossed in that activity…when time passes in a vacuum as you hone in with razor-sharp focus and clarity toward a triumphal moment? It is likely you will have several things you enjoy doing, so much so that they create this state. These are your passions. Once you have found them, brainstorm ways in which you can make a living by working within your passion. It may require some creative thinking or even moderate risk-taking, but if there is a will, there is a way.

Even if your passion goes undiscovered or you are unable to make a living from it, hard work will still get you to the goal of financial freedom. It may not be as easy or as enjoyable, but it is still achievable.

A few other concepts that financially successful people adhere to and recommend when it comes to work include these:

- Don't take too much time contemplating things. Start your activity and things will begin to fall into place. Go for it. Just do it. Be a "doer."

- If something seems impossible, simply break it into smaller, more manageable, less intimidating tasks and start with the first one. With time, tackling those small tasks one by one will add up to you achieving the "impossible" task you were intimidated by initially.

- A willingness to change and adapt is crucial. Doing the same things will keep you at your current level of financial success. You have to do something different, you have to grow, and you have to take risks in order to achieve your goals.

- Once you are on your path and working hard, persevere, be persistent, be determined, don't quit, keep your head down, and keep moving forward. Stay focused on your goal. Keep growing, gaining experience, and developing your skills. Have confidence that you can work through any obstacles or troubles that present themselves. Be bold, courageous, determined, and willing to sacrifice.

Review the following quotes to reinforce the importance of finding your passion and working hard at it.

In the long run you won't be successful at something you don't enjoy doing. Enjoyment is an indispensable ingredient for success. We are successful at the things we enjoy, the endeavors we love, the labors we are excited and passionate about.

- Matthew Kelly

The only way to be truly satisfied is to do what you believe is great work. And the only way to do great work is to love what you do. If you haven't found it yet, keep looking. Don't settle. As with all matters of the heart, you'll know when you find it.

- Steve Jobs

Nothing great was ever achieved without enthusiasm.

- Ralph Waldo Emerson

Only those who dare to fail greatly can ever achieve greatly.

- Robert Kennedy

One secret of success in life is for a man to be ready for his opportunity when it comes.

- Benjamin Disraeli

Look at a stone cutter hammering away at his rock, perhaps a hundred times without as much as a crack showing in it. Yet at the hundred-and-first blow it will split in two, and I know it was not the last blow that did it, but all that had gone before.

- Jacob A. Riis

In creating, the only hard thing is to begin: a grass blade's no easier to make than an oak.

- James Russell Lowell

Your success in life will be in direct proportion to what you do after you do what you are expected to do.

- Brian Tracy

The only difference between a rich person and a poor person is what they do in their spare time…What you do after work with your paycheck and your spare time will determine your future.

- Robert Kiyosaki

In this age, which believes that there is a short cut to everything, the greatest lesson to be learned is that the most difficult way is, in the long run, the easiest.

- Henry Miller

Find a job you like and you add five days to every week.

- H. Jackson Brown, Jr.

He who wishes to be rich in a day will be hanged in a year.

- Leonardo da Vinci

Every extraordinary accomplishment is the result of thousands of ordinary accomplishments that no one recognizes or appreciates.

- Brian Tracy

The person who really wants to do something finds a way; the other finds an excuse.

- From a sign posted in Ramalho's West End Gym in Lowell, Massachusettes

Discover Your Passion and Work Hard

You've got to follow your passion. You've got to figure out what it is you love—who you really are. And have the courage to do that. I believe that the only courage anybody ever needs is the courage to follow your own dreams.

- Oprah Winfrey

The dictionary is the only place that success comes before work.

- Vince Lombardi

Desire is the key to motivation, but it's determination and commitment to an unrelenting pursuit of your goal—a commitment to excellence—that will enable you to attain the success you seek.

- Mario Andretti

If you go on doing what you have always done, you'll go on getting what you've always got.

- Dr. Lair Ribeiro

Everything comes to him who hustles while he waits.

- Thomas Edison

Choose a job you love, and you will never have to work a day in your life.

- Confucius

...seek to solve bigger problems...because inside of big problems lie huge financial opportunities.

- Robert Kiyosaki

There is no substitute for hard work.

- Thomas Edison

The difference in winning and losing is most often...not quitting.

- Walt Disney

Opportunities are usually disguised as hard work, so most people don't recognize them.

- Ann Landers (Esther P. Lederer)

Things may come to those who wait, but only the things left by those who hustled.

- Abraham Lincoln

When I was a young man I observed that nine out of ten things I did were failures. I didn't want to be a failure, so I did ten times more work.

- George Bernard Shaw

People rarely succeed unless they have fun in what they are doing.

- Dale Carnegie

If you observe a really happy man, you will find him building a boat, writing a symphony, educating his son, growing double dahlias in his garden, or looking for dinosaur eggs in the Gobi desert. He will not be searching for happiness as if it were a collar button that has rolled under the radiator.

- W. Beran Wolfe

We act as though comfort and luxury were the chief requirements of life, when all that we need to make us really happy is something to be enthusiastic about.

- Charles Kingsley

Early to bed and early to rise, makes a man healthy, wealthy, and wise.

- Benjamin Franklin

Nothing is particularly hard if you divide it into small jobs.

- Henry Ford

In the business world, everyone is paid in two coins: cash and experience. Take the experience first; the cash will come later.

- Harold S. Geneen

Instead of living below your means, focus on increasing your means.

- Robert Kiyosaki

He is well paid that is well satisfied.

- William Shakespeare, *The Merchant of Venice*

Just don't give up trying to do what you really want to do. Where there is love and inspiration, I don't think you can go wrong.

- Ella Fitzgerald

It takes 20 years to make an overnight success.

- Eddie Cantor

Opportunity is missed by most people because it is dressed in overalls and looks like work.

- Thomas Edison

Five frogs are sitting on a log. Four decide to jump off. How many are left? Answer: Five. Why? Because there is a difference between deciding and doing.

- Mark L. Feldman & Michael F. Spratt

My father always told me, "Find a job you love and you'll never have to work a day in your life."

- Jim Fox

Luck is a dividend of sweat. The more you sweat, the luckier you get.

- Ray Kroc

The three great essentials to achieve anything worthwhile are, first, hard work; second, stick-to-itiveness; third, common sense.

- Thomas Edison

The darkest day in a man's career is that wherein he fancies there is some easier way of getting a dollar than by squarely earning it.

- Horace Greeley

Don't go into business with the sole objective of making a lot of money. If you put service, quality, and customer satisfaction first—the money will follow.

- Paul Clitheroe

Regardless of if you work for someone else or for yourself, if you want to be rich, you've got to mind your own business. And in minding your own business, the plan that works best for you will slowly appear. So take your time, yet keep taking one step a day and you will have a good chance of getting everything you want in your life.

- Robert Kiyosaki

When everything seems to be going against you, remember that the airplane takes off against the wind, not with it.

- Henry Ford

Your greatest and most powerful business survival strategy is going to be the speed at which you handle the speed of change. That speed of change is trend.

- Ajaero Tony Martins

Often people attempt to live their lives backwards, they try to have more things or more money in order to do more of what they want so that they will be happier. The way it actually works is the reverse. You must first be who you really are then do what you need to do in order to have what you want.

- Margaret Young

Money will come when you are doing the right thing.

- Mike Phillips

What we really want to do is what we are really meant to do. When we do what we are meant to do, money comes to us, doors open for us, we feel useful, and the work we do feels like play to us.

- Julia Cameron

Every day I get up and look through the Forbes list of the richest people in America. If I'm not there, I go to work.

- Robert Orben

A business has to be involving, it has to be fun, and it has to exercise your creative instincts.

- Richard Branson

The man who will use his skill and constructive imagination to see how much he can give for a dollar, instead of how little he can give for a dollar, is bound to succeed.

- Henry Ford

Empty pockets never held anyone back. Only empty heads and empty hearts can do that.

- Norman Vincent Peale

If money is your hope for independence you will never have it. The only real security that a man will have in this world is a reserve of knowledge, experience, and ability.

- Henry Ford

Passions are wired into the real world more directly than our workday routines are. If you love something, you'll bring so much of yourself to it that it will create your future.

- Francis Ford Coppola

Nothing happens by itself…it all will come your way, once you understand that you have to make it come your way, by your own exertions.

- Ben Stein

To gain more abundance a person needs more skills and needs to be more creative and cooperative. People who are creative, have good financial and business skills, and are cooperative often have lives of increasing financial abundance.

- Robert Kiyosaki

Money never starts an idea. It is always the idea that starts the money.

- Owen Laughlin

The supreme accomplishment is to blur the line between work and play.

- Arnold Toynbee

Desire! That's the one secret of every man's career. Not education. Not being born with hidden talents. Desire.

- Bobby Unser

Genius is one percent inspiration, ninety-nine percent perspiration.

- Thomas Edison

If you put all your strength and faith and vigor into a job and try to do the best you can, the money will come.

- Lawrence Welk

It is the working man who is the happy man. It is the idle man who is the miserable man.

- Benjamin Franklin

Pursuing your passion is fulfilling and leads to financial freedom.

- Robert G. Allen

Notoriety and a fat bank balance must come after everything else is finished and done.

- Ray Bradbury

The sleeping fox catches no poultry.

- Benjamin Franklin

No one who can rise before dawn 360 days a year fails to make his family rich.

- Chinese Proverb

Opportunities multiply as they are seized.

- Sun Tzu

I don't know that there are any shortcuts to doing a good job.

- Sandra Day O'Connor

Follow your instincts. That's where true wisdom manifests itself.

- Oprah Winfrey

Never mistake motion for action.

- Ernest Hemingway

The world belongs to the energetic.

- Ralph Waldo Emerson

If you work just for money, you'll never make it, but if you love what you're doing and you always put the customer first, success will be yours.

- Ray Kroc

What we have to learn to do, we learn by doing.

- Aristotle

One very important aspect of motivation is the willingness to stop and to look at things that no one else has bothered to look at. This simple process of focusing on things that are normally taken for granted is a powerful source of creativity.

- Edward de Bono

One who walks in another's tracks leaves no footprints.

- Proverb

Motivation is what gets you started. Habit is what keeps you going.

- Jim Rohn

Motivation is like food for the brain. You cannot get enough in one sitting. It needs continual and regular top ups.

- Peter Davies

Just as appetite comes from eating, so work brings inspiration, if inspiration is not discernible at the beginning.

- Igor Stravinsky

To bring one's self to a frame of mind and to the proper energy to accomplish things that require plain hard work continuously is the one big battle that everyone has. When this battle is won for all time, then everything is easy.

- Thomas A. Buckner

Do not worry if you have built your castles in the air. They are where they should be. Now put the foundations under them.

- Henry David Thoreau

That's why many fail—because they don't get started—they don't go. They don't overcome inertia. They don't begin.

- W. Clement Stone

The master in the art of living makes little distinction between his work and his play, his labor and his leisure, his mind and his body, his information and his recreation, his love and his religion. He hardly knows which is which. He simply pursues his vision of excellence at whatever he does, leaving others to decide whether he is working or playing. To him he is always doing both.

- James Michener

Don't follow your dreams; chase them.

- Richard Dumb

Do your work with your whole heart and you will succeed—there's so little competition.

- Elbert Hubbard

There is no scarcity of opportunity to make a living at what you love. There is only a scarcity of resolve to make it happen.

- Dr. Wayne Dyer

The only 'break' anyone can afford to rely upon is a self-made 'break.'

- Napoleon Hill

Doing what you love is the cornerstone of having abundance in your life.

- Wayne Dyer

Whatever you can do, or dream you can, begin it. Boldness has genius, power, and magic in it.

- Johann Goethe

If you're trying to achieve, there will be roadblocks. I've had them; everybody has had them. But obstacles don't have to stop you. If you run into a wall, don't turn around and give up. Figure out how to climb it, go through it, or work around it.

- Michael Jordan

Nothing splendid has ever been achieved except by those who dared believe that something inside them was superior to circumstances.

- Bruce Barton

If you believe in yourself and have the courage, the determination, the dedication, the competitive drive, and if you are willing to sacrifice the little things in life and pay the price for the things that are worthwhile, it can be done.

- Vince Lombardi

Nothing stops the man who desires to achieve. Every obstacle is simply a course to develop his achievement muscle. It's a strengthening of his powers of accomplishment.

- Eric Butterworth

It's not the hours you put in your work that counts, it's the work you put in the hours.

- Sam Ewing

The secret of getting ahead is getting started. The secret of getting started is breaking your complex overwhelming tasks into small manageable tasks, and then starting on the first one.

- Mark Twain

Some people want it to happen, some wish it would happen, others make it happen.

- Michael Jordan

Don't aim for success if you want it; just do what you love and believe in, and it will come naturally.

- David Frost

Whatever you are by nature, keep to it; never desert your line of talent. Be what nature intended you for, and you will succeed.

- Sydney Smith

Persistent people begin their success where others end in failure.

- Edward Eggleston

Heaven ne'er helps the men who will not act.

- Sophocles

I hated every minute of training, but I said, 'Don't quit. Suffer now and live the rest of your life as a champion.'

- Muhammad Ali

The critical ingredient is getting off your butt and doing something. It's as simple as that. A lot of people have ideas, but there are few who decide to do something about them now. Not tomorrow. Not next week. But today. The true entrepreneur is a doer, not a dreamer.

- Nolan Bushnell

If you are willing to do only what's easy, life will be hard. But if you are willing to do what's hard, life will be easy.

- T. Harv Eker

Work is a surefire money-making scheme.

- Dave Ramsey

Formal education will make you a living; self education will make you a fortune.

- Jim Rohn

Great works are performed not by strength but by perseverance.

- Samuel Johnson

You are never given a wish without also being given the power to make it come true. You may have to work for it, however.

- Richard Bach

Always bear in mind that your own resolution to succeed is more important than any other one thing.

- Abraham Lincoln

There are no traffic jams on the extra mile.

- Zig Ziglar

Diamonds are only lumps of coal that stuck to their jobs.

- B.C. Forbes

Obstacles are those frightful things you see when you take your eyes off your goal.

- Henry Ford

Nothing in this world can take the place of persistence. Talent will not; nothing is more common than unsuccessful men with talent. Genius will not; unrewarded genius is almost a proverb. Education will not; the world is full of educated derelicts. Persistence and determination alone are omnipotent. The slogan "Press on" has solved and will always solve the problems of the human race.

- Calvin Coolidge

I can summarize the lessons of my life in seven words—never give in; never, never give in.

- Winston Churchill

I do not think that there is any other quality so essential to success of any kind as the quality of perseverance. It overcomes almost everything, even nature.

- John D. Rockefeller

Success seems to be connected with action. Successful men keep moving. They make mistakes, but they don't quit.

- Conrad Hilton

Nothing in this world that's worth having comes easy.

- Dr. Bob Kelso (*Scrubs* TV show)

I'm a great believer in luck, and I find the harder I work, the more I have of it.

- Thomas Jefferson

When I have fully decided that a result is worth getting, I go ahead on it and make trial after trial until it comes. Nearly every man who develops an idea works it up to the point where it looks impossible, and then he gets discouraged. That's not the place to become discouraged.

- Thomas Edison

What this power is I cannot say; all I know is that it exists and it becomes available only when a man is in that state of mind in which he knows exactly what he wants and is fully determined not to quit until he finds it.

- Alexander Graham Bell

Remember, you can only make so much money with your hands. How much you can make with your brain is unlimited.

- Peter H. Thomas

You will get all you want in life, if you help enough other people get what they want.

- Zig Ziglar

4

SMART SPENDING

Thinking about and tracking how you spend money is another key attribute that many individuals who have achieved financial freedom exert. Many preach the importance of spending less than you earn and having the self-discipline to delay gratification until you have the money in your pocket.

A few other applicable methods they teach include these:

1. Do not worry about appearance and just spending to look wealthy.

2. Be cognizant of all your expenses, even the little ones, because they add up!

Review the quotes in this chapter to keep you focused on spending smart. Yes, you need to spend money on the basics and you should enjoy your money, but doing this in a smart way will help you attain the most important thing: piece of mind.

The next time you are debating whether or not to spend your money on some item, browse through this chapter to help you determine whether or not to make that purchase.

The amount of money you have has got nothing to do with what you earn. People earning a million dollars a year can have no money and people earning $35,000 a year can be quite well off. It's not what you earn, it's what you spend.

- Paul Clitheroe

Annual income twenty pounds, annual expenditure nineteen [pounds] nineteen [shillings] and six [pence], result happiness. Annual income twenty pounds, annual expenditure twenty pounds ought and six, result misery.

- Charles Dickens

I don't think you can spend yourself rich.

- George Humphrey

Thousands upon thousands are yearly brought into a state of real poverty by their great anxiety not to be thought poor.

- Robert Mallett

Dollars do better if they are accompanied by sense.

- Earl Riney

A budget is telling your money where to go instead of wondering where it went.

- John Maxwell

Wealth is what you accumulate by living well below your means.

- Thomas J. Stanley & William D. Danko

Beware of little expenses; a small leak will sink a great ship.

- Benjamin Franklin

The riskiest of all investors are those who have nothing but liabilities they think are assets, have as much in expenses as they have in income, and whose only source of income is their labor.

- Robert Kiyosaki

The art of living easily as to money is to pitch your scale of living one degree below your means.

- Sir Henry Taylor

Smart Spending

Men do not understand how great a revenue is economy.

- Cicero

We make ourselves rich by making our wants few.

- Henry David Thoreau

If you can, you will quickly find that the greatest rate of return you will earn is on your own personal spending. Being a smart shopper is the first step to getting rich.

- Mark Cuban

There are plenty of ways to get ahead. The first is so basic I'm almost embarrassed to say it: spend less than you earn.

- Paul Clitheroe

Financial peace isn't the acquisition of stuff. It's learning to live on less than you make, so you can give money back and have money to invest. You can't win until you do this.

- Dave Ramsey

Budget: a mathematical confirmation of your suspicions.

- A.A. Latimer

The study wanted to find out how people born into poverty eventually become wealthy. The study found that these people...possessed three qualities. These qualities were:
1. They maintained a long term vision and plan.
2. They believed in delayed gratification.
3. They used the power of compounding in their favor.

- Robert Kiyosaki

My problem lies in reconciling my gross habits with my net income.

> -   Errol Flynn

Never spend your money before you have it.

> -   Thomas Jefferson

If you know how to spend less than you get, you have the philosopher's stone.

> -   Benjamin Franklin

He who will not economize will have to agonize.

> -   Confusius

A bargain ain't a bargain unless it's something you need.

- Sidney Carroll

Being frugal does not mean being cheap! It means being economical and avoiding waste.

- Catherine Pulsifer

Act your wage.

- Dave Ramsey

It's not your salary that makes you rich, it's your spending habits.

- Charles A. Jaffe

Don't tell me where your priorities are. Show me where you spend your money and I'll tell you what they are.

- James W. Fick

Too many people spend money they haven't earned, to buy things they don't want, to impress people they don't like.

- Will Rogers

5

DEBT

Debt is something that many who have achieved great wealth avoid. Some avoid debt altogether—others use it only when they can profit from it.

The key is to understand the differences between good debt and bad debt. In some areas and at some point in your life, you may need to take on some form of debt (e.g., purchase a new home, build a business, etc.). In other areas, you should never have debt, such as credit cards, if you cannot pay them off every month. As you will see in this chapter, many of these individuals consider debt to be on par with slavery because when you are in debt, you limit your options.

Do you currently carry debt? Don't worry; just take time to set up a plan to eliminate it, and then follow that plan without worry.

So the next time you pull out the credit card to make a purchase, make sure you have 100% of the money to pay it once the bill comes due; otherwise, pull out this book and review the quotes below.

He that goes a-borrowing goes a-sorrowing.

- Benjamin Franklin

You want 21 percent risk free? Pay off your credit cards.

- Andrew Tobias

Don't stretch yourself too much with a mortgage. Buy within your means...it's not worth the sleepless nights.

- Sarah Beeny

Debt

Credit buying is much like being drunk. The buzz happens immediately and gives you a lift.... The hangover comes the day after.

- Joyce Brothers

Some debts are fun when you are acquiring them, but none are fun when you set about retiring them.

- Ogden Nash

What can be added to the happiness of a man who is in health, out of debt, and has a clear conscience?

- Adam Smith

It is the debtor that is ruined by hard times.

- Rutherford B. Hayes

Rather go to bed supperless, than rise in debt.

- Benjamin Franklin

Debt, n. An ingenious substitute for the chain and whip of the slavedriver.

- Ambrose Bierce

No man's credit is as good as his money.

- E.W. Howe

Bad debt is sacrificing your future day needs for your present day desires.

- Suze Orman

Debt

Live within your means, never be in debt, and by husbanding your money you can always lay it out well. But when you get in debt you become a slave. Therefore I say to you never involve yourself in debt, and become no man's surety.

- Andrew Jackson

Before borrowing money from a friend, decide which you need more.

- Addison H. Hallock

The second vice is lying, the first is running in debt.

- Benjamin Franklin

When a man is in love or in debt, someone else has the advantage.

- Bill Balance

Debt

A man in debt is so far a slave.

> \- Ralph Waldo Emerson

Creditors have better memories than debtors.

> \- Benjamin Franklin

There are but two ways of paying debt: increase of industry in raising income, increase of thrift in laying out.

> \- Thomas Carlyle

He...looks the whole world in the face. For he owes not any man.

> \- Henry Wadsworth Longfellow

Debt is the worst poverty.

> \- Thomas Fuller

Do not accustom yourself to consider debt only as an inconvenience; you will find it a calamity.

> \- Samuel Johnson

Debt is dumb. Cash is king.

> \- Dave Ramsey

Debt can turn a free, happy person into a bitter human being.

> \- Michael Mihalik

If you're thinking of debt, that's what you're going to attract.

- Bob Proctor

Debt is normal. Be weird.

- Dave Ramsey

Home life ceases to be free and beautiful as soon as it is founded on borrowing and debt.

- Henrik Ibsen

Wouldst thou shut up the avenues of ill, Pay every debt as if God wrote the bill.

- Ralph Waldo Emerson

6

SAVING

It takes discipline to reach your financial goals—the discipline to watch your spending and to save regularly. One of the best habits of those who have reached financial independence is to save a certain percentage of every dollar they earn. Ten percent is the amount many recommend. Of course, if you can afford to go above 10%, say to 15% or 20%, that's even better. For anyone just starting out, you can do as little as 2%. The key is to get in the habit of putting a percentage of your earnings aside as soon as you receive it. Don't wait until the end of the month and save whatever you have left—pay yourself first!

What is this money being saved for? The financially successful people usually recommend it be used for two things:

1. An emergency fund. This is an amount of money that will cover a certain number of months of living expenses (6–12 months typically) in case something happens and you have no money coming in.

2. A financial independence fund. The money you put in this fund you will never spend. It is money that is set aside to work for you by producing passive income. This account will continue to grow and grow. One day, it will be producing enough passive income to cover all of your expenses. That is the day you will no longer have to work; your money will be doing all the work for you!

Reference the quotes below to keep you motivated to consistently save money in your emergency and financial independence funds.

Gold cometh gladly and in increasing quantity to any man who will put by not less than one-tenth of his earnings to create an estate for his future and that of his family.

- George S. Clason

Saving

Rich people plan for four generations. Poor people plan for Saturday night.

- Gloria Steinem

Wealth can only be accumulated by the earnings of industry and the savings of frugality.

- John Tyler

If you would be wealthy, think of saving as well as getting.

- Benjamin Franklin

It's never too early to encourage long-term savings.

- Ron Lewis

Saving

Anything that we can do to raise personal savings is very much in the interest of this country.

- Alan Greenspan

Money grows on the tree of patience.

- Proverb

Save a part of your income and begin now, for the man with a surplus controls circumstances and the man without a surplus is controlled by circumstances.

- Henry H. Buckley

All days are not same. Save for a rainy day. When you don't work, savings will work for you.

- M.K. Soni

Personally, I tend to worry about what I save, not what I spend.

- Paul Clitheroe

A penny saved is a penny earned.

- Benjamin Franklin

A penny here, and a dollar there, placed at interest, goes on accumulating, and in this way the desired result is attained. It requires some training, perhaps, to accomplish this economy, but when once used to it, you will find there is more satisfaction in rational saving than in irrational spending.

- P. T. Barnum

A simple fact that is hard to learn is that the time to save money is when you have some.

- Joe Moore

Saving

The safe way to double your money is to fold it over once and put it in your pocket.

- Kin Hubbard

You must learn to save first and spend afterwards.

- John Poole

It is thrifty to prepare today for the wants of tomorrow.

- Aesop

On the first day of every week each one of you is to put aside and save, as he may prosper.

- Corinthians 16:2

Saving

The time to save is now. When a dog gets a bone, he doesn't go out and make a down payment on a bigger bone. He buries the one he's got.

> \- Will Rogers

Don't spend your life working for money; save money and hire it to work for you.

> \- Dr. John F. Demartini

The reason saving comes before investing is that you need to have seed before you can sow it in anticipation of a harvest.

> \- Rajen Devadason

The art is not in making money, but in keeping it.

> \- Proverb

Saving

If saving money is wrong, I don't want to be right.

- William Shatner

One should save money so that his future is secured and he does not have to worry at the time of need. One, who does not this will always be on the mercy of others.

- Sam Veda

The way to build your savings is by spending less each month.

- Suze Orman

The test is simple and infallible. Are you able to save money? If not, the seed of success is not in you.

- James J. Hill

7

INVESTING

Once you are spending smart, out of debt, and regularly saving money, you need to find something beneficial to do with that money. This is where investing comes in. All those who are financially well-off invest their money to make it grow.

If you listen to many of those who have achieved financial independence, they will tell you a lot of the same things in regard to investing as the great minds who authored the quotes below. They will tell you that you have to: (1) take risks, (2) have specific objectives for the money and a plan for your investments, (3) invest in something you know well and understand, (4) understand that there will be lows in the market, (5) keep your emotions in check, and (6) don't gamble or speculate.

Yet, as you will see below, there are differences of opinion in some instances. For example, some of these individuals recommend diversifying your investments while others suggest focusing your investment on something you know really, really well.

The quotes below provide great investing advice.

Bull markets are born on pessimism, grow on skepticism, mature on optimism, and die on euphoria.

- Sir John Templeton

Investing is a popularity contest, and the most dangerous thing is to buy something at the peak of its popularity. At that point, all favorable facts and opinions are already factored into its price, and no new buyers are left to emerge.

- Howard Marks

The market can remain irrational longer than you can remain solvent.

- John Maynard Keynes

…keep your earned income secure by purchasing a security you hope converts your earned income into passive income or portfolio income.

- Robert Kiyosaki

To buy when others are despondently selling and to sell when others are euphorically buying takes the greatest courage, but provides the greatest profit.

- Sir John Templeton

There are two kinds of people who lose money: those who know nothing and those who know everything.

- Henry Kaufman

There are old investors, and there are bold investors, but there are no old bold investors.

- Howard Marks

The investor's chief problem—and even his worst enemy—is likely to be himself.

- Benjamin Graham

I have made a resolution to let my money work instead of me.

- John D. Rockefeller

There are two times in a man's life when he should not speculate: when he can't afford it and when he can.

- Mark Twain

Investing

Never invest in any idea you can't illustrate with a crayon.

- Peter Lynch

You only have so many hours in a day and you can only work so hard. So why work hard for money. Learn to have money and people work hard for you, and you can be free to do the things that are important.

- Robert Kiyosaki

Successful investing is anticipating the anticipations of others.

- John Maynard Keynes

Wide diversification is only required when investors do not understand what they are doing.

- Warren Buffett

Throughout all my years of investing I've found that the big money was never made in the buying or the selling. The big money was made in the waiting.

- Jesse Livermore

If you hear that everybody is buying a certain stock, ask who is selling.

- James Dines

October. This is one of the peculiarly dangerous months to speculate in stocks. The others are July, January, September, April, November, May, March, June, December, August, and February.

- Mark Twain

Money doesn't bring courage, I learned. It's the other way around.

- Suze Orman

Sometimes your best investments are the ones you don't make.

- Donald Trump

Because ensuring the ability to survive under adverse circumstances is incompatible with maximizing returns in the good times, investors must choose between the two.

- Howard Marks

Never do business or invest for tax reasons. A tax break is an extra bonus for doing things the way the government wants. It should be a bonus, not the reason.

- Robert Kiyosaki

Money is a terrible master but an excellent servant.

- P.T. Barnum

Success in investing doesn't correlate with I.Q. once you're above the level of 25. Once you have ordinary intelligence, what you need is the temperament to control the urges that get other people into trouble in investing.

- Warren Buffett

The four most expensive words in the English language are, 'This time it's different.'

- Sir John Templeton

Investing should be more like watching paint dry or watching grass grow. If you want excitement, take $800 and go to Las Vegas.

- Paul Samuelson

In investing, what is comfortable is rarely profitable.

- Robert Arnott

How many millionaires do you know who have become wealthy by investing in savings accounts? I rest my case.

- Robert G. Allen

Bottoms in the investment world don't end with four-year lows; they end with 10- or 15-year lows.

- Jim Rogers

The individual investor should act consistently as an investor and not as a speculator.

- Benjamin Graham

It's not how much money you make, but how much money you keep, how hard it works for you, and how many generations you keep it for.

- Robert Kiyosaki

You get recessions, you have stock market declines. If you don't understand that's going to happen, then you're not ready, you won't do well in the markets.

- Peter Lynch

If investing is entertaining, if you're having fun, you're probably not making any money. Good investing is boring.

- George Soros

If you have trouble imagining a 20% loss in the stock market, you shouldn't be in stocks.

- John Bogle

If I'd only followed CNBC's advice, I'd have a million dollars today. Provided I'd started with a hundred million dollars.

- Jon Stewart

To be successful as an investor or a business owner, you have to be emotionally neutral to winning and losing. Winning and losing are just part of the game.

- Robert Kiyosaki

I rarely think the market is right. I believe non-dividend stocks aren't much more than baseball cards. They are worth what you can convince someone to pay for it.

- Mark Cuban

In this business if you're good, you're right six times out of ten. You're never going to be right nine times out of ten.

- Peter Lynch

When buying shares, ask yourself, would you buy the whole company?

- Rene Rivkin

Investing

It's one of the most important things at the end of the day, being able to say no to an investment.

- Henry Kravis

Most of the time common stocks are subject to irrational and excessive price fluctuations in both directions as the consequence of the ingrained tendency of most people to speculate or gamble... to give way to hope, fear and greed.

- Benjamin Graham

I've found that when the market's going down and you buy funds wisely, at some point in the future you will be happy. You won't get there by reading 'Now is the time to buy.'

- Peter Lynch

An investor without investment objectives is like a traveler without a destination.

- Ralph Seger

…never…become addicted to the idea of a high-paying job…develop the thought pattern of thinking only in assets and income in the form of capital gains, dividends, rental income, residual income from businesses and royalties.

- Robert Kiyosaki

Based on my own personal experience—both as an investor in recent years and an expert witness in years past—rarely do more than three or four variables really count. Everything else is noise.

- Marty Whitman

Know what you own, and know why you own it.

- Peter Lynch

Never count on making a good sale. Have the purchase price be so attractive that even a mediocre sale gives good results.

- Warren Buffett

Investing

The way to make money is to buy when blood is running in the streets.

- John D. Rockefeller

The wise man puts all his eggs in one basket and watches the basket.

- Andrew Carnegie

Your boss's job is to give you a job. It's your job to make yourself rich.

- Robert Kiyosaki

Buy when everyone else is selling and hold until everyone else is buying. This is not merely a catchy slogan. It is the very essence of successful investing.

- J. Paul Getty

Investing

Go to the mouse you foolish investor and learn. A mouse never entrusts its life to only one hole.

- Ajaero Tony Martins

When stocks are attractive, you buy them. Sure, they can go lower. I've bought stocks at $12 that went to $2, but then they later went to $30. You just don't know when you can find the bottom.

- Peter Lynch

Business opportunities are like buses, there's always another one coming.

- Richard Branson

There is a very easy way to return from a casino with a small fortune: go there with a large one.

- Jack Yelton

If past history was all there was to the game, the richest people would be librarians.

- Warren Buffett

Nobody ever lost money taking a profit.

- Bernard Baruch

Go for a business that any idiot can run—because sooner or later, any idiot probably is going to run it.

- Peter Lynch

If a business does well, the stock eventually follows.

- Warren Buffett

...don't invest until you have a plan. Always remember that investing is a plan...not a product or procedure.

- Robert Kiyosaki

Do you know the only thing that gives me pleasure? It's to see my dividends coming in.

- John D. Rockefeller

I will tell you the secret to getting rich on Wall Street. You try to be greedy when others are fearful. And you try to be fearful when others are greedy.

- Warren Buffett

8

FINAL THOUGHTS

Let's face it, money is an important aspect of our lives. You need if for both basic necessities like food and shelter, and to do many of the things that make life so enjoyable, such as travel or giving to others. Yet, the wisest of the wise will remind you that money is not <u>the</u> most important thing. They will remind you to keep a practical perspective, appreciate what you have, and take time to slow down and enjoy life.

It is important to work hard and stay focused on your goals, but not so much that you forget to enjoy your life's journey. Don't compare your life to others' and enjoy, appreciate, and celebrate what you have.

Don't get too caught up in these lessons that you forget to enjoy the wealth you have amassed, for a large amount of money is not the ultimate goal.

Final Thoughts

The goal is to not have to worry about money, to do the things you enjoy, and to help others with that wealth. For this is truly what we seek and what ultimately enriches our lives.

Use the quotes below to help you keep your journey to financial freedom in perspective.

The Dalai Lama, when asked what surprised him most about humanity, answered, "Man. Because he sacrifices his health in order to make money. Then he sacrifices money to recuperate his health. And then he is so anxious about the future that he does not enjoy the present; the result being that he does not live in the present or the future; he lives as if he is never going to die, and then dies having never really lived."

- Dalai Lama

Do not spoil what you have by desiring what you have not; remember that what you now have was once among the things you only hoped for.

- Epicurus

Happiness doesn't depend on what we have, but it does depend on how we feel toward what we have. We can be happy with little and miserable with much.

- William Dempster Hoard

Wealth is not his that has it, but his that enjoys it.

- Benjamin Franklin

You're only here for a short visit, so don't hurry, don't worry. And be sure to smell the flowers along the way.

- Walter C. Hagen

Enjoy your own life without comparing it with that of another.

- Marquis de Condorcet

So many people spend their health gaining wealth, and then have to spend their wealth to regain their health.

- A.J. Reb Materi

A wise man should have money in his head, but not in his heart.

- Jonathan Swift

Focusing your life solely on making a buck shows a poverty of ambition. It asks too little of yourself. And it will leave you unfulfilled.

- Barack Obama

Money will buy you a fine dog, but only love can make it wag its tail.

- Richard Friedman

Men for the sake of getting a living forget to live.

- Margaret Fuller

If money be not thy servant, it will be thy master. The covetous man cannot so properly be said to possess wealth, as that may be said to possess him.

- Francis Bacon

Happiness is making the most of what you have.

- Rosamunde Pilcher

It is good to have an end to journey toward; but it is the journey that matters, in the end.

- Ursula K. LeGuin

Final Thoughts

All other good gifts depend on time for their value. What are friends, books, or health, the interest of travel or the delights of home, if we have not time for their enjoyment? Time is often said to be money, but it is more—it is life; and yet many who would cling desperately to life, think nothing of wasting time.

- Sir John Lubbock

Riches are for spending.

- Francis Bacon

Money is like manure. You have to spread it around or it smells.

- J. Paul Getty

The true worth of a man is to be measured by the objects he pursues.

- Marcus Aurelius

Be content with what you have; rejoice in the way things are. When you realize there is nothing lacking, the whole world belongs to you.

- Lao Tzu

The fastest way to bring more wonderful examples of abundance into your personal experience is to take constant notice of the wonderful things that are already there.

- Esther Hicks

Have fun in your command. Don't always run at a breakneck pace. Take leave when you've earned it: Spend time with your families. Corollary: surround yourself with people who take their work seriously, but not themselves, those who work hard and play hard.

- Colin Powell

An aim in life is the only fortune worth finding.

- Robert Louis Stevenson

Happiness consists more in small conveniences or pleasures that occur every day, than in great pieces of good fortune that happen but seldom.

- Benjamin Franklin

Happiness is to be found along the way, not at the end of the road, for then the journey is over and it is too late. Today, this hour, this minute is the day, the hour, the minute for each of us to sense the fact that life is good, with all of its trials and troubles, and perhaps more interesting because of them.

- Robert R. Updegraff

Make money your god and it will plague you like the devil.

- Henry Fielding

Final Thoughts

The highest use of capital is not to make more money, but to make money do more for the betterment of life.

- Henry Ford

Money is like love; it kills slowly and painfully the one who withholds it, and enlivens the other who turns it on his fellow man.

- Kahlil Gibran

I know of nothing more despicable and pathetic than a man who devotes all the hours of the waking day to the making of money for money's sake.

- John D. Rockefeller

Final Thoughts

After you become a millionaire, you can give all of your money away because what's important is not the million dollars; what's important is the person you have become in the process of becoming a millionaire.

- Jim Rohn

It's good to have money and the things that money can buy, but it's good, too, to check up once in a while and make sure that you haven't lost the things that money can't buy.

- George Lorimer

WE WANT TO HEAR FROM YOU

Here at My Life Coaches, Inc. we measure our success by the number of lives our products positively impact. If this book, and the words within it, have impacted your life in a positive way, please share your story with us. You can email us at contact@mylifecoaches.com.

All individuals who share their stories are entered into a quarterly drawing for a free gift.

GIVE THE GIFT OF FINANCIAL FREEDOM

Would someone in your life benefit from the words in this book? If so, you can order additional copies of this book, or any of the other books in the Inspirational Quotes for Your Life Series by contacting us at contact@mylifecoaches.com. Volume discounts are available.

www.ingramcontent.com/pod-product-compliance
Lightning Source LLC
Chambersburg PA
CBHW051715170526
45167CB00002B/665